SLOANE STEPHENS

Get in the game with your favorite athletes:

BECKY SAUERBRUNN

TAMBA HALI

KEVIN DURANT

SLOANE STEPHENS

REAL SPORTS
CONTENT NETWORK PRESENTS

SLOANE
STEPHENS
Craig Ellenport

ALADDIN

NEW YORK LONDON TORONTO SYDNEY NEW DELHI

ALADDIN

An imprint of Simon & Schuster Children's Publishing Division
1230 Avenue of the Americas, New York, New York 10020
First Aladdin hardcover edition November 2019

For information about special discounts for bulk purchases, please contact
Simon & Schuster Special Sales at 1-866-506-1949 or business@simonandschuster.com.
The Simon & Schuster Speakers Bureau can bring authors to your live event. For more
information or to book an event contact the Simon & Schuster Speakers Bureau
at 1-866-248-3049 or visit our website at www.simonspeakers.com.
Series designed by Greg Stadnyk
Interior designed by Tom Daly
The text of this book was set in Caecilia LT Std.
Manufactured in the United States of America 1019 FFG
2 4 6 8 10 9 7 5 3 1
Library of Congress Control Number 2019939316
ISBN 978-1-4814-8226-4 (hc)
ISBN 978-1-4814-8225-7 (pbk)
ISBN 978-1-4814-8227-1 (eBook)

CONTENTS

SLOANE STEVENS: The Basics   1

CHAPTER 1: The US Open Champ   5

CHAPTER 2: Florida to Fresno
              (and Back Again)   16

CHAPTER 3: Tennis Prodigy   23

CHAPTER 4: Back-to-Back Losses   28

CHAPTER 5: On the Rise   38

CHAPTER 6: Beating Serena   46

CHAPTER 7: Chasing Her First Title   62

CHAPTER 8: Dealing with Injury   71

CHAPTER 9: Grand Slam and Beyond   80

CHAPTER 10: Helping Others   88

CHAPTER 11: Sloane's Legacy   97

SOURCES   105

SLOANE STEPHENS

SLOANE STEPHENS: THE BASICS

BIRTHDAY: March 20, 1993

HOMETOWN: Fort Lauderdale, Florida

TENNIS BACKGROUND: It's common to hear stories of tennis stars picking up a racquet for the first time as soon as they learn to walk. However, Sloane Stephens didn't start playing until she was nine years old, when she started hitting balls while watching her mother's tennis lesson. But it didn't take long for everyone to see she was a natural.

COLLEGE: Stephens took online courses and graduated in 2017 from Indiana University East with a bachelor's degree in communications.

SHORT LIST OF TENNIS ACHIEVEMENTS: Stephens has won seven titles—six in the WTA (Women's Tennis Association) and one in the ITF (International Tennis Federation). She has won one of the four major events known as "Grand Slam" events. That was the 2017 US Open. In the other Grand Slam events, her best finishes were: semifinals at the Australian Open (2013); quarterfinals at Wimbledon (2013); and finals at the French Open (2018). By the end of 2018, her career prize money was more than $13 million.

US NATIONAL TEAM: Stephens represented the United States in the 2016 Olympics in Rio de Janeiro, Brazil. She lost in the first round to Canada's Eugenie Bouchard.

HER MANTRA: "Whatever happens, happens." There have been several times in her career when tennis commentators have questioned Stephens's desire, her passion for the game. They don't like the fact that she doesn't seem to get very upset when she loses. But it's just part of her even-keeled outlook. "Obviously, nobody's perfect and it doesn't always go your way," she says. "You can't get too down with losses and you can't get too high with wins. You have to have a good balance."

WHAT YOU REALLY NEED TO KNOW ABOUT HER: Stephens loves to prepare food. She was inspired to cook by her grandmother, Gloria, who gave her a handwritten list of all her special recipes for her eighteenth birthday. "Cooking is so peaceful," Stephens says. "No TV, no phone, just me and my ingredients." According to Stephens's mother, she makes an incredible apple pie.

CHAPTER 1

THE US OPEN CHAMP

What does a professional tennis player do on the eve of a major championship match? If you're Sloane Stephens, the night before your first appearance in the final of one of the sport's four biggest events—the 2017 US Open—you are in your New York City hotel room, reading online car safety reviews.

Of course.

Was the twenty-four-year-old Stephens looking to buy a car? No. But she was bored, and nervous. She didn't want to talk to friends or family, didn't want to get lost in a movie. So she sat quietly in her room, browsing Autotrader.com for no apparent reason.

Okay, so maybe that's not what all professional tennis players do the night before a huge tournament. It's probably safe to say Sloane Stephens is the *only* professional tennis player who's ever done that. But then again, that's just one of many ways in which Stephens is unlike most other professional tennis players.

On the one hand, anybody would be nervous going into their first big championship match, on such a big stage. On the other hand, it could be argued that Stephens was already a big winner just getting *this* far. After all, when the 2017 US Open tournament began in late August of that year, Stephens was ranked eighty-third in the Women's Tennis Association (WTA).

And that was not bad, considering where she'd been ranked earlier that summer.

Number 957.

Nine hundred fifty-seven!

Who knew there were that many women professional tennis players?

Actually, there had been a time when Stephens was ranked much higher. It was true, she had never reached the final of one of the Grand Slam events, but she had been a successful figure in women's tennis for more than five years. The reason she had such a low ranking in the summer of 2017 was that she had been out of competition, fighting her way back after foot surgery that had her temporarily in a wheelchair.

Overall, she was off the courts for eleven months, slowly working her way back into form. By the time she got to Queens, New York, for the US Open, Stephens was on a roll. She had won fourteen of her last sixteen matches coming into the Open.

When she won her first-round match—defeating

2015 US Open finalist Roberta Vinci—it was her first victory at the US Open since 2014. In the second round, she beat No. 11 seed Dominika Cibulkova. Two days later she defeated Ashleigh Barty, an up-and-coming young Australian player. In the fourth round, she took care of No. 30, Julia Görges, to reach the quarterfinals.

The quarterfinal match against No. 16, Anastasija Sevastova of Latvia, marked Stephens's first match ever on center court at Arthur Ashe Stadium. The crown jewel of the Billie Jean King National Tennis Center, which hosts the US Open, Arthur Ashe Stadium is the largest tennis stadium in the world. Literally and figuratively, it is the biggest stage in the sport, and Stephens was up to her first challenge there. She defeated Sevastova, 6–3, 3–6, 7–6, to earn a date with Venus Williams in the semifinals.

The other semifinal match featured Madison Keys and CoCo Vandeweghe—which was significant.

For the first time in thirty-six years, all four women's semifinalists at the US Open were American.

That was well and good, but Stephens's primary concern was getting past Venus Williams—a player Stephens had idolized when she was younger—to reach her first Grand Slam final.

Venus and Serena Williams were the dominant figures in women's tennis in the twenty-first century. Serena would go on to win more Grand Slam titles than anyone in the modern era, but it was older sister Venus who burst on the scene first. By the time Stephens was eight years old, Venus had already won the US Open twice.

Because of their success on the tennis court, the Williams sisters were arguably among the most successful and recognizable African American women in the world, which made it easy for an African American girl like Sloane Stephens to grow up admiring them.

Stephens still admired and appreciated all that

Venus and Serena had accomplished, but she could no longer let those feelings get in the way of her own ambitions. This was not the first time she'd face one of the Williams sisters—her victory over Serena in the 2013 Australian Open quarterfinals was the match that put Stephens squarely on the tennis map—but this contest was huge as well.

When the match began, it looked like it would be easy: Stephens took the first set, 6–1. But just as she breezed through that set, Williams made quick work of the second set, winning 6–0.

In the best-of-three match, Stephens shook off that poor second set to win the first two games of the third and deciding set. But then the roller-coaster ride began: Williams won the next three games to go up 3–2; Stephens won the next two to go up 4–3; Williams took the next two for a 5–4 lead.

The tenth game was tied 30–30. Stephens was two points away from tying the set—but she was also two points away from losing the match. She decided she was not going to lose.

On the ensuing volley, Stephens rocketed a backhand shot down the line that flew past Williams. Stephens won the next point too, and the set was all tied up. In the eleventh game, Stephens made a perfect drop shot—that means putting spin on the ball so it drops just over the net and is impossible for a player standing back at the baseline to get to it in time—breaking Williams's serve and taking a 6–5 lead in the set.

Suddenly Stephens found herself serving for the match. Four points later, she had it. The 6–1, 0–6, 7–5 victory sent her to the US Open final.

Despite the momentous win over Williams in the semifinals, Stephens still found herself nervously reading those car safety reviews in the hotel on the eve of the title match.

But when it came time to face her good friend Madison Keys in the US Open championship match the next day, Stephens was cool, calm, and collected. Unlike the quarterfinal win over Sevastova or the semifinal win over Williams, the final didn't require a third set.

Stephens won the first set, 6–3. She was up 4–0 in the second set but facing game point. Keys made a great drop shot, but Stephens came racing to the net and returned the volley. With Stephens at the net, Keys was in position to easily hit a forehand shot over her head to close out the game, but Stephens—using lightning-fast reflexes—lunged to her right and sent the ball back over the net. With Keys back by the baseline, she had no chance to get to it. The game went to deuce and Stephens then won the game to go up 5–0—putting her on the brink of a title.

With Stephens up 6–3, 5–0, Keys fought off two match points as game six went to deuce. Stephens won the next point—and for the third time reached championship point. After a long volley, Keys hit a forehand that slammed into the net.

Game. Set. Match.

Stephens lifted both arms in triumph as she walked toward the net. Then her eyes opened wide and she covered her mouth with her left hand. It slowly sank in what she had just accomplished. She hugged Keys, her good friend, then made her way up to her box and shared a long embrace with her mother.

Stephens was the fourteenth unseeded player to advance to a Grand Slam final in the Open era (only the top 32 in the rankings are seeded among the 128 players at the Open).

"When I had surgery, I was not thinking that I would be anywhere near a US Open title," she said after the match. "Nor did I think I was going to be anywhere near the top hundred."

Ranked No. 83 going into the US Open, she was the lowest-ranked player ever to win the event. Two days after her victory, when the rankings were updated, Stephens was No. 17 in the world.

"I mean, there are no words to describe how I got here, the process it took or anything like that," she said. "Because if you told someone this story, they'd be, like, 'That's insane.'"

Stephens became just the fourth African American woman ever to win a Grand Slam singles title, following in the footsteps of three legendary players: Althea Gibson, Serena Williams, and Venus Williams.

It was a crowning achievement for Stephens, who had overcome many obstacles on and off the court to reach this point. She had battled multiple injuries, answered to critics who had questioned her desire to win, weathered a public feud with the biggest star in her sport, and dealt with family tragedy.

Because of all those things, the post-match embrace she shared with her mother was so special.

"My whole life my mom has been very supportive," she said. "She's been in my corner the whole time, and I have had, you know, a lot of ups and a lot of downs—and some really low downs. And throughout that, my mom has been there one hundred percent with me."

CHAPTER *2*

FLORIDA TO FRESNO (AND BACK AGAIN)

Sloane Stephens was born on March 20, 1993, in Plantation, Florida, a small city in South Florida just west of Fort Lauderdale. It was never guaranteed that she would grow up to be a professional athlete, but she certainly started with a bit of an advantage.

Children of great athletes often inherit the genes that helped their parents become so physically gifted. In Stephens's case, she had a pair of impressive gene pools to draw upon.

Her mother, Sybil Smith, is still recognized as the

greatest swimmer in the history of her college, Boston University. She set seven school records there that stand today. In 1988, by virtue of finishing sixth in the hundred-yard backstroke at the NCAA Championships, she was named a First Team All-American. More than just a stellar achievement, it was a significant milestone: Smith became the first African American woman ever to earn All-America honors in the sport. She graduated in 1988 and was inducted into the Boston University Hall of Fame in 1993.

Sloane's father, John Stephens, was a professional football player. The same year that Smith was named an All-American, John Stephens was selected by the New England Patriots in the first round of the National Football League draft. Stephens, a running back from Shreveport, Louisiana, who played college football at Northwestern State in Louisiana, quickly became a star in the NFL. He ran for 1,168 yards in 1988 and was named the NFL's Offensive Rookie of the Year.

At six foot one and 215 pounds, Stephens possessed a unique combination of speed and strength. His first coach with the Patriots, Hall of Fame player Raymond Berry, said he was one of the best athletes he had ever seen. Berry compared him to one of the greatest running backs in NFL history, Jim Brown.

In other words, Sloane had a head start in her development as an athlete.

"She's got a good gene pool," her uncle, Tony Smith, once said of Sloane. "But she's taken it to a whole other level. It just makes me so proud to know what she's accomplished and where she came from."

That said, DNA was about all she got from her father when she was growing up.

John Stephens's NFL career faded almost as quickly as it had taken off. In 1989 he had a head-on collision in a game against the San Francisco 49ers that left the player who tackled him partially paralyzed. It wasn't Stephens's fault, but he was never the same player after that. Whether or not that was the reason, Stephens didn't seem to run as hard as he did in his rookie season. His rushing yards dropped each year and by 1991 he was a backup, being used more as a blocker than a runner.

His last season in the NFL was 1993, which was a significant year in his life for a different reason: it was the year his daughter was born.

A year after her birth, he and Sybil Smith were divorced. John moved back to his home state of Louisiana, and Sybil was left to raise Sloane as a single parent.

Because Smith needed help raising her baby daughter, the two moved across the country, back to her childhood home in Fresno, California, in the northern part of that state. They lived in a house with Smith's parents.

While Smith went to graduate school—studying to become a psychologist—a young Stephens spent plenty of time with her grandfather, who had come to America from Trinidad. Although he'd grown up in poverty in Trinidad, he earned a college scholarship and became a doctor in his adopted United States.

In 1997 Sybil Smith remarried, and Sloane had a new father figure in her life. His name was Sheldon Farrell, and he raised Sloane as if she were his own.

Farrell was an avid tennis player, and as luck would have it, the family lived across the street from the Sierra Sport & Racquet Club. Farrell was a member there and he played tennis all the time. When Sloane was nine years old, her mother took lessons there.

Sloane herself wasn't all that interested in playing competitively, but sometimes she would tag along with her mother and hit tennis balls against the wall to kill time during her mother's lesson.

As it turned out, she was a natural.

Francisco Gonzalez, a former professional tennis player, was one of the coaches at Sierra Sport & Racquet Club. Gonzalez represented Paraguay as a pro in the 1970s and '80s. He was never ranked higher than No. 34 in the world, but he was good enough to record victories over past champions such as Ivan Lendl, Jimmy Connors, and Stefan Edberg.

It was Gonzalez who first recognized that Stephens was special. He taught her the game, coached her, and encouraged her to begin playing in competitions.

"She progressed so fast," said Gonzalez. "She was beating kids that had been probably playing longer than she had. She used her speed to move around the court."

Most tennis prodigies are introduced to the sport at a much younger age, but Stephens's athleticism, coordination, and feel for the sport helped her advance at an extraordinary pace.

Before long, Gonzalez came to the realization

that Stephens was good enough that she could have a promising career playing tennis. But if that was to be the case, then she needed to be elsewhere. In order to advance to the next level, he told Sybil Smith and Sheldon Farrell, the family needed to move back to South Florida. It was there, he told them, that Sloane could get the best training and preparation for a professional career in tennis.

And so, at age ten, Sloane and family moved to Fort Lauderdale.

CHAPTER 3

TENNIS PRODIGY

Upon the family's return to South Florida, Sloane joined the Evert Tennis Academy, an elite facility in Boca Raton that was cofounded by successful tennis pro John Evert and his sister, legendary tennis champion Chris Evert.

John Evert had developed and managed several top juniors, college players, and professionals over the years, but it didn't take long before young Sloane advanced to the point where she required more attention than she could get at the Evert Tennis Academy.

Her next stop: the Nick Saviano High Performance Tennis Academy. Located in Plantation, where Sloane was born, the Saviano High Performance Tennis Academy has one of the best reputations in the country when it comes to producing professional tennis players. The "Saviano method" is taught exclusively at this academy, and the rigorous schedule includes six days a week of training. Stephens was playing tennis four hours a day and doing physical training and conditioning one hour a day.

"That's when I really got into it just with fitness and tennis," Stephens said. "I started playing a lot more."

The schedule became very demanding, however, and it was cutting into her schoolwork. The decision was made that it would be better if Stephens were homeschooled.

"I was missing a lot of school for tournaments and they would drop your grade a letter," she recalled.

"I was missing so much, it was just easier wh(
can do it by yourself and get help that way,
than missing school and not getting any hel]
you're away."

By 2006, when she was just thirteen, St
began competing in low-level events on th
national Tennis Federation (ITF) Junior
In the summer of 2008, she won her firs1
sional title—an ITF doubles tournament in
Kansas. Her doubles partner was Christin;
who trained at the nearby USTA Training
Boca Raton, Florida.

Later that year, Stephens had her fir:
success on a bigger stage. She reached th
the 2008 US Open Girls' Doubles tourna
Mallory Burdette, who also attended t
High Performance Tennis Academy.

In December, Stephens entered the
Bowl, a Grade A juniors event in Sout}
singles competition. "Grade A" events

weight than other tournaments when calculating player rankings. She reached the semifinals, where she lost a three-set match to her former doubles partner Christina McHale.

Not yet sixteen years old, Stephens was getting acclimated to big-time tennis competition. She continued to play doubles, but it was the singles competition—where there was no one to rely on but herself—where Stephens thrived.

"I actually love that tennis is an individual sport," Stephens told ExperienceLife.com in 2013. "I welcome the added pressure of being alone on the court because that pressure is what makes tennis one of the best sports in the world. I have found that the best way to psychologically prepare for pressure situations is to just admit that nerves are part of the game. I'm definitely not one of those players who claim they don't get nervous."

It's one thing for Stephens to be able to compete

on a tennis court, turning that pressure into positive energy and blocking out potential distractions. Off the court, however, there were a few major developments in her life that would be impossible to ignore.

CHAPTER 4

BACK-TO-BACK LOSSES

Needless to say, Sloane Stephens's tennis success was a constant source of pride for both her mother and Sheldon Farrell, her stepfather. After all, he was the one who had introduced her to the sport in the first place.

Watching Sloane's career develop and taking her to training sessions and tournaments was a happy diversion for the family—because at the same time, there was also a very difficult situation to be dealt with.

It wasn't long after the family relocated to Fort

Lauderdale in 2003 that Farrell was diagnosed with terminal cancer. At the same time Stephens was making a name for herself on the Junior Circuit, Farrell battled his cancer for two and a half years. In late 2007, sadly, he died.

Understandably, Stephens was devastated.

"For Sloane, her stepdad was really connected to her tennis, so when he passed away, she didn't even want to play," said her mother, Sybil Smith. "Sloane had to grow up really fast."

Smith was always there for support. Stephens was also close with her younger half brother, Shawn Farrell. And as fate would have it, there would be another family member back on the scene just when he was needed most: Sloane's biological father.

Even though John Stephens hadn't seen his daughter since she was a baby, he'd followed her early success as a rising tennis prodigy. And he was very proud.

Sloane's success was one of the few things John could be happy about. He had led a troubled life in the years since his NFL days. The most recent issue proved to be quite serious: John learned that he had a degenerative bone disease. His mortality fueled a desire to spend time with the daughter he'd never known.

With Sybil's consent, John reached out to Sloane in 2006, when she was thirteen. After a few phone conversations, Sloane went to visit her father for the first time at his home in Louisiana. She also got to meet John's mother—Sloane's grandmother—and a few of John's other children by another woman—Sloane's half-siblings.

While the reunion was certainly awkward, it didn't take long for father and daughter to bond. Smith always said that Sloane's vivacious personality and penchant for smiling were traits she clearly inherited from her father.

"She's got his charisma; it's kind of bizarre,"

Smith told ESPN the Magazine. "Talk about inheritance: she's just like the guy, and she didn't meet him until she was thirteen."

For the next three years, Stephens didn't see her father, but the two spoke often on the phone.

"It was all good," she recalled years later. "All good memories. I'm glad I had the time to get to know him and I'm glad we became friends."

John Stephens loved getting updates from Sloane as she began to make a name for herself on the Junior Circuit.

She won the singles and doubles titles at the USTA International Spring Championships in 2009. Mallory Burdette was her doubles partner. She won the Grade A Italian Open.

Also in 2009, Sloane entered the French Open Junior Championships for the first time. It was the first time she had played in a junior championship at one of the four Grand Slam events—the biggest events in all of tennis. The four Grand Slam tournaments are the Australian Open, the French Open, Wimbledon (in England), and the US Open.

To her credit, Stephens reached the semifinals at the French Open, then lost to Kristina Mladenovic, who went on to win the title. A few weeks later, she made her debut at the Wimbledon Juniors, reaching the quarterfinals.

In the summer of 2009, Stephens was in New York preparing for the US Open Juniors tournament when she got a call from one of her half sisters. John Stephens had been in a car accident in Louisiana. His pickup truck had skidded off a dark, winding road and struck a tree.

Two years after the death of her stepfather, Sloane Stephens got the news that her biological father, John Stephens, was dead.

"Right after she found out, she cried for about an hour and a half," her mother told the *New York Times*. After that, she went out to hit tennis balls, something that helped as both practice for the tournament and distraction from the tragic news she had just heard.

But now a decision had to be made. Sloane's first match in the Juniors competition was Sunday, September 6. Her father's funeral was scheduled for Tuesday, September 8, in Louisiana. Should she go?

John Stephens would have told his daughter not to leave New York for the funeral. Her career was too important, he would have said, and this was the US Open. But Stephens wanted to be there, to see her father one last time.

"I told her she's free to do whatever she wants to do," her mother said at the time. "I think right now she feels that the safest place for her is on the tennis court."

After agonizing over the decision, she managed to get to the funeral without missing any tennis. She won her first-round match, went to the funeral, then returned to New York to face Maryna Zanevska of Ukraine in a second-round match.

Showing surprising composure given the circum-
stances, Stephens prevailed in three sets, 7–6, 3–6,
6–2. Two days later she lost in a third-round match.

"On the court it's not so bad, but off the court
it's rough," said Stephens, who had a large con-
tingent of family and friends on hand to provide
moral support during the match. "Focusing on the
court is pretty easy, but sometimes it gets to you."

If the news of her father's death was painful,
what was to follow would be a gut punch.

Since finally reuniting with him as a thirteen-
year-old, Stephens could always call her father if
she had any questions. Now that he was gone, she
wanted to learn all she could about him. After the
US Open ended, she took to the Internet to learn
more. Unfortunately, what she discovered was not
good.

It was at this time that she found out that John
Stephens had been arrested and charged with rape
in Missouri in 1994. That was the reason Sybil Smith

left him in the first place. He had pleaded guilty and was placed on probation at the time. Sloane later learned that in April of 2009, John Stephens was charged with sexual assault in Louisiana. Those charges were still pending when he was killed.

Sloane was devastated, but Sybil Smith never regretted her decision not to tell her daughter about John's troubled past.

"I wanted her to have pride in him," Smith said. "I'm telling you, John was a very good man with addiction issues that were never addressed early on."

As a rookie with the New England Patriots in 1988, John Stephens had been honored by the NFL for his work with the Roxbury Comprehensive Community Health Center. His teammates all said he was one of the nicest guys on the team. He was always smiling and always there for a friend in need. When he reached out to Smith in 2006 about wanting to connect with Sloane, Smith did her homework—talking to people down in Louisiana, who confirmed that he was still the caring, friendly person she had married.

"It's very sad," she said, "because Sloane and her dad became so close. They had a great friendship. She knew a part of her dad that was all good and she was able to be proud of him."

Smith didn't know about the more recent sexual assault charges, which didn't occur until well after John had reconnected with Sloane.

"When he passed away, it really became evident that he still had some serious issues," Smith said, adding that she thinks Sloane has come to terms with her father's troubled past. "But I think those questions will linger for her lifetime," she said, "because she never got a chance to say, 'Dad, what's up with this?'"

Stephens can't ignore her father's troubled past, but she chooses to remember him as the good man she got to know just a little. She can appreciate that she inherited his elite athletic ability—not to mention his beaming smile and pleasant disposition.

"I wish he could come to a tournament and see my play now," Stephens told *Time* magazine before the 2018 US Open. "I know he's there. He's watching."

CHAPTER **5**

ON THE RISE

It's easy for fans to forget that all celebrities—professional athletes, musicians, movie stars—have the same real-life issues that they do. So when Stephens had to deal with losing her stepfather and her biological father within two years, tennis fans may not have realized she was having a hard time focusing on her sport.

In fact, Stephens went through a phase in which tennis just wasn't fun for her.

"It was a really tough time in her life, and both losses were incredibly overwhelming," Stephens's mother told *American Way* magazine. "She had to really find that passion for tennis again and compartmentalize those feelings."

Stephens was only sixteen years old when her father died and she learned about his troubled past. It's the kind of experience that forces a teenager to grow up in a hurry.

"I feel like I'm already fifty-five and lived a whole life because I had been through all those things," she told *Time* magazine in 2013. "I've definitely learned to handle myself better."

Perhaps it was a result of what she had just been through, but Stephens woke up one morning in October of 2009, just one month after her father died, and made another life-changing decision: it was time to turn pro.

Because of age restrictions in the Women's Tennis Association (WTA), Stephens was limited in the number of professional tournaments she could play each year. So as 2010 began, she split time between competing as a pro in the WTA and continuing a successful run on the Junior Circuit.

In the Juniors, 2010 was a year to remember. Partnering with Timea Babos of Hungary, Stephens won the Juniors girls' doubles championships in all three of the Grand Slam tournaments they entered: the French Open, Wimbledon, and the US Open. They were only the second girls' doubles team ever to win three Grand Slam titles in one year, the first to do it in fifteen years.

Stephens fared well in the Juniors singles competition as well. She didn't win any of the majors, but she reached at least the quarterfinals in the three Grand Slam events in which she participated. Her best result was a semifinal appearance at the US Open.

Her limited pro experience in 2010 began in March, when she qualified for the prestigious Indian Wells Open in Southern California just days before her seventeenth birthday. In her first career match as a pro, Stephens faced Lucie Hradecka of the Czech Republic. The first two sets were hard-fought contests that both required tiebreaks, but Stephens prevailed in both, winning the match 7–6, 7–6. Her second-round match was against Russian Vera Zvonareva, who was ranked twelfth in the world at the time. Stephens played well but lost in straight sets, 6–4, 7–5.

Her only other WTA event in 2010 came at the Swedish Open, and she again won her first-round match before losing in the second round. But as a seventeen-year-old with two pro wins under her belt, Stephens was on her way. After starting the year ranked No. 802 in the world, she finished 2010 ranked in the top two hundred, at No. 198.

If 2010 was a small taste of success for Stephens, 2011 was a full-course meal. By the time she arrived at the 2011 Camparini Gioielli Cup tournament in Italy, she was ranked No. 151 in the world. Entering the tournament as the sixth seed, she defeated second-seed Sabine Lisicki in the semifinals and then breezed past Anastasiya Yakimova, 6–3, 6–1, in the final. On May 15, at age eighteen, Sloane Stephens for the first time was crowned a professional tennis champion.

Later that month, even with a championship on her résumé, Stephens still had to battle through the qualifying rounds to earn a spot in the 2011 French Open. She was successful in the qualifier but lost a first-round match to Elena Baltacha. Still, just reaching the main draw of a major helped lift her world ranking to No. 128.

Stephens's climb continued. In August she defeated No. 20, Julia Görges, on the way to her first quarterfinal appearance at a WTA event, the Mercury Insurance Open in Carlsbad, California. One month later she was awarded a wild-card spot in the US Open, her first appearance as a pro at the final Grand Slam tournament of the year. In the first round, she defeated Réka Luca Jani for her first career Grand Slam match victory. She followed that with a second-round win over No. 23, Shahar Pe'er. Stephens lost in round three to Serbian star Ana Ivanovic, ranked No. 16 at the time, but her two wins at the Open vaulted her into the top 100—making her the youngest player in the WTA's top 100.

Stephens's 2012 season began with her first appearance at the Australian Open, where she won her first-round match before losing in round two. Stephens competed in all four Grand Slam events in 2012, and that second-round loss at the Australian was actually her earliest exit of the four. At the French Open, she reached the fourth round before losing to Sam Stosur, who was ranked No. 6 in the world. At Wimbledon, she upset No. 23 seed, Petra Cetkovska, to reach the third round before losing to No. 15 seed, Sabine Lisicki. At the US Open, her final event of the year, she lost in the third round to Ana Ivanovic.

When she lost at the US Open, few people knew

that Stephens had actually been playing in pain for months. Back at the French Open in the spring, Stephens tore her abdominal muscle. But she didn't want to miss key events during the summer, so she played through the injury. In particular, she was really hoping to make the US National Team, which would compete in the 2012 Summer Olympics. She was the fifth-highest ranked American at the time—the bad news was that only the top four earned the trip to London.

Following her loss at the Open, Stephens found herself having to deal with a new problem.

"After I lost to Ivanovic, people were like, 'Oh, she wasn't trying,' and I was like, 'I'm definitely bleeding in my abdomen and going to the hospital.' They gave me all this medicine to make it go down, and they thought I had a blood clot. Whatever, obviously I'm alive now, so it's fine."

While recovering from that injury, she spent time "going to football games, hanging out with friends, and being nineteen." She also worked more on her conditioning than ever before.

By the end of 2012, Stephens reached another milestone in the WTA rankings. She was now up to No. 38 in the world—at age nineteen, the youngest player in the top fifty.

Stephens earned $400,000 in prize money in 2012—not bad for any nineteen-year-old, but she was just scratching the surface of what she could become. The money didn't faze her—Stephens never spent a lot of money on anything other than food. She was still getting an allowance from her mother, and that was just fine. Even though she didn't compete in the final three months of the year while she recovered from the abdominal injury, it seemed as if Stephens was ready to do something big.

"I'm ranked thirty-eight now, so that can only get better," she said at the time. "I think I have a lot of things to bring in 2013. It'll all work out, you'll see. It will be really, really good."

CHAPTER 6

BEATING SERENA

As Stephens prepared to begin the 2013 tennis season with a trip to Australia, she was fully healed from the abdominal injury that had plagued her in the second half of 2012. More important, she was happy and focused on her game.

"This is probably the first time Sloane's gone into a season saying, 'I can't wait to get out there and play,'" her mother told ABC News.

Stephens's first tournament of 2013 was the Brisbane International, an event in Queensland that is a warm-up to the Australian Open, the first Grand Slam event of the year. Stephens breezed through the first two rounds of the tournament, setting up a third-round match against the No. 3 player in the world—Serena Williams.

This would be the first time Stephens had faced Williams, the younger of the record-breaking sisters she'd grown up idolizing. Williams had been the No. 1 player in the world on multiple occasions, and she was already considered one of the best women's tennis players of all time. The only reason she wasn't the top-ranked player at this point was because she had missed a lot of time in 2010 and 2011 while fighting through injuries. But as 2013 began, it was clear to all that she was back at the top of her game.

Williams had lost in the first round of the 2012 French Open, but she was lights-out from that point on. In a display of dominance, she won Wimbledon in July, then captured a gold medal at the 2012 Olympics in August. She breezed through the US Open in September and finished 2012 with a title at the WTA Finals.

So it really came as no surprise that Williams defeated Stephens in straight sets in that first-ever meeting at the Brisbane International. Still, the champ had high praise for her challenger. After the match, Williams told reporters that Stephens could be "the best in the world one day."

Despite the loss, Stephens's showing at Brisbane lifted her high enough in the rankings that she entered the Australian Open one month later as the tournament's twenty-ninth seed. It was the first time she was seeded in a Grand Slam event, and she backed up her seeding by cruising through the first four rounds to reach the quarterfinals of a Grand Slam for the first time. Her reward: another meeting with Serena Williams.

By this point, Williams was on a twenty-match winning streak. Needless to say, Stephens went into the Australian quarterfinals as a heavy underdog.

That just meant she had nothing to lose. When she woke up on the morning of the match, Stephens said to herself, "Look, dude, like, you can do this. Like, just go out and play and do your best."

Stephens would lose the first set, 6–3. She served the first game of the second set, but Williams broke her. Would this be another quick straight-sets loss to her idol?

"I was like, 'Hmm, this is not the way you want it to happen,'" Stephens recalled telling herself at that point. "'But you just fight and just get every ball back, run every ball down, and just get a lot of balls in play, I think you'll be okay.' From then on, I got aggressive, started coming to the net more, and just got a lot more comfortable."

As Stephens got more comfortable, Williams was actually in great pain. In the eighth game of that second set, Williams hurt her back chasing a drop shot. She had to take a medical time-out after the set, which Stephens won, 7–5. Her back had locked up on her and it was clear the pain—not to mention the stiff competition from Stephens—was bothering her. At one point in the match, Williams slammed her racquet into the ground, smashing it. She was cited for racquet abuse. Stephens, meanwhile, maintained her composure.

In the third set, the two competitors held serve (winning the games they served) through the first six games, tied 3–3. Then Serena broke for a 4–3 lead. That could have been the beginning of the end, but Stephens broke right back to tie the set at 4–4. She held serve for a 5–4 lead and then broke Williams one more time to clinch the stunning victory.

Everybody loves an underdog, so the crowd at Rod Laver Arena was solidly behind Stephens. They knew they had just witnessed a coming-out party, of sorts. The victory put Stephens on the map as a rising young star in the world of women's tennis.

Stephens was still in disbelief at what she had just accomplished when she was interviewed on the court after the match. During the match, the broadcasters talked a lot about the poster of Serena Williams that Stephens had in her room as a child. She was asked about it after the match.

Stephens smiled shyly. "I think I'll put up a poster of myself now," she said. The crowd ate it up.

A win like this would profoundly affect Stephens's life in many different ways, but one of the first things she thought about was something that was top of mind for most teenagers at the time—whether or not they were professional athletes: social media.

In particular, Stephens was hooked on Twitter. After checking how many Twitter followers she had following the match, she gleefully proclaimed: "It was seventeen thousand, and now I have thirty-five thousand!" (Stephens now has more than two hundred thousand followers.)

In addition to all the text messages she received from family and friends, the Twitter world chimed in as well. She got hundreds of tweets from people congratulating her, including some from celebrities. Shaquille O'Neal sent her this message:

When u defeat a legend, you become a legend. Keep it going.

Two days after Stephens's stunning victory over Williams, she lost in the semifinals to Victoria Azarenka, the defending Australian Open champion, 6–1, 6–4, but that did little to diminish what she had achieved in Australia. When the updated WTA rankings were released after the tournament, Stephens shot up to No. 17 in the world— she was the youngest player in the top twenty.

The tennis world had taken notice. When ABC News ran a feature on Stephens after her victory against Williams, the on-screen graphic read:

TEEN TENNIS CINDERELLA BEATS HER IDOL.

"That put her on the map worldwide," says former player Mary Joe Fernandez. "If you have a big win or get far in a major, then all of a sudden it's instant recognition."

Hall of Fame tennis legend Chris Evert had high praise. "When it comes to the next generation of American players, Sloane is ahead of everybody," Evert said. "Her court coverage is exceptional; she's a great ball striker."

Of course, with all the new attention on her, Stephens began to hear the inevitable comparisons. Truth be told, it wasn't really new. A rising young female tennis player—who happens to be African American—is quite obviously going to be compared to Venus and Serena Williams, who had been the dominant forces in women's tennis for more than a decade.

It made perfect sense: Stephens grew up idolizing Venus and Serena, and the fact that her biggest victory to date came against one of them only added to the story line. In the days and weeks following her big win at the Australian Open, there were countless stories written with headlines like THE NEXT SERENA and HEIRESS APPARENT.

Stephens would have none of it.

"Of course it's a compliment to be compared to one of the greatest champions the sport has ever seen, but I actually think it's pretty ridiculous that I'm compared to Serena," Stephens said during an interview with ExperienceLife.com. She pointed out that at the time she had a total of zero Grand Slam titles to her name while Williams had seventeen (she has since raised that total to twenty-three Grand Slam singles titles, an all-time record). Stephens wasn't even in the top ten yet, while Williams had been ranked No. 1 in the world on multiple occasions. Recognizing that she had a long way to go to match Williams's achievements, Stephens insisted that the comparisons were not adding any stress.

"It doesn't add more pressure because I don't look at myself as the next Serena," she said. "I am my own person, and I will be the next Sloane Stephens."

I will be the next Sloane Stephens.

It was a good quote, and she probably meant it. But there was no denying that the onslaught of Sloane-Serena comparisons were causing anxiety and stress. Maybe that wasn't the only reason Stephens struggled in her matches following the Australian Open, but it was definitely a factor. She lost four of her next seven matches.

The fourth loss in that stretch came in March 2013 in the fourth round of the Miami Open. And in the post-match press conference, the frustration started to show.

"I mean, it's just a rough time. I don't know," she said when asked about the slump. "There's no specific thing that I'd say has happened or is not happening, but I don't think it really matters."

After reaching No. 17 in the world, she figured

she could afford to lose a few more matches and still be somewhere around the top thirty.

"I'm not really too concerned about winning or losing or any of that, I don't think. My life has changed, yeah, but I wouldn't say I'm in a panic or anything."

Once again, the criticisms about Stephens not caring enough began to surface. When you're out there on the tennis court by yourself, people want to see blood and sweat . . . but also tears. They didn't want to hear Stephens say, "It's all good" after losing a match. They wanted her to get mad. The fact of the matter is, outside observers had no way of knowing what Stephens was thinking or feeling. Just because she didn't wear her emotions on her sleeve didn't mean she didn't care.

That said, there was a distraction that was affecting her in this current slump.

In the days following that loss in Miami, she opened up to ESPN the Magazine about the Serena issues, and it was clear that was weighing on her. She referred to a tweet from Williams two days after their match in Australia in which Williams said, "I made you." Stephens said she knew the tweet was directed at her. More notably, she said she basically has had no relationship with Williams since their match.

"She's not said one word to me, not spoken to me, not said hi, not looked my way, not been in the same room with me since I played her in Australia," Stephens told ESPN the Magazine. "And that should tell everyone something, how she went from saying all these nice things about me to unfollowing me on Twitter."

Stephens chalked up the hype to zealous media that wanted to focus on the fact that they are both African American. Still, everyone remembered the story about that Serena Williams poster Stephens had hanging in her room as a child. What about that?

Stephens told ESPN the Magazine a story about the poster that was previously unknown. Turns out when Stephens was twelve, her mother took her to a tennis event in Delray Beach in which both Williams sisters were playing. Stephens brought the poster and waited after the event to get the posted signed.

She waited. And waited. And even when Serena did pass by, she didn't stop to sign anything.

"They walked by three times and never signed our posters," Stephens said. She told ESPN the Magazine that's when she adopted a new favorite player.

"I'm annoyed. I'm over it," she said. "I've always said Kim Clijsters is my favorite player, so it's kind of weird."

So there it was. No matter who started it or why, Stephens clearly had launched the latest attack in this very public Sloane-Serena rivalry.

In the ESPN the Magazine story, the writer

was interviewing Stephens and her mother, Sybil Smith, together. And when Stephens started telling the story about the poster, her mother actually tried to discourage her from getting into it. Smith knew it would only make matters worse, but her daughter didn't care.

Next up on the WTA tour was a trip to Europe for the Madrid Open in May. It was a first-round loss for Stephens, but the good news was that the trip signified an end to the feud with Williams, just as it was getting so public.

The tension between the two star tennis players began to ease when Williams was asked by reporters after her second-round match at the Madrid Open about Stephens's comments in the ESPN the Magazine story. Williams expressed only praise for Stephens.

"I don't really know. I don't have many thoughts," she said. "I'm a big Sloane Stephens fan and always have been. I've always said that I think she can be the best in the world. I'll always continue to think that and always be rooting for her."

Williams's comments were soon followed by a tweet from Stephens in which she accepted responsibility for the strained relations and extended an olive branch:

> *Guilty of being naive. Much respect*
> *4 @serenawilliams, a champ &*
> *the GOAT. We spoke, we're good.*
> *ONWARD! #lifelessons.*

The tennis world was glad to see this public spat fade away.

Great to see @serenawilliams & @sloanetweets have talked & figured it out, tweeted broadcaster and former tennis star Tracy Austin. *Not easy to grow up in front of world & do everything perfectly!*

The Sloane-Serena saga may not have been the only reason why Stephens went through a slump after the Australian Open, but ending the feud did prove to be a positive turning point. In late May,

Stephens went to Roland-Garros for the French Open—the second major of the year—and reached the fourth round before losing to Maria Sharapova, who was ranked No. 2 in the world at the time. It was the first time she had won three straight matches since her run at the Australian Open.

For her part, Sharapova—who had been through plenty of ups and downs and off-the-court drama in her career—had very nice things to say about Stephens following their match.

"There are some players you play against and you're not quite sure if they will be able to develop something to a different level," Sharapova told reporters. "But I think there's a lot of room for a few things to improve, and I think she will. . . . This is a really important time in her career. If she's in the right hands at the right time, I'm sure she's going to have a great career."

CHAPTER 7

CHASING HER FIRST TITLE

Only halfway through the year, 2013 was already a wild ride when Sloane Stephens arrived in London in late June for Wimbledon, the third Grand Slam of the season. First had come the groundbreaking win over Serena Williams in the Australian Open quarterfinals in February. Then there was the public feud with Williams, which accompanied a terrible slump. Finally Stephens got back on track at the French Open.

The positive trajectory continued at Wimbledon, where she won four matches—including three straight hard-fought three-setters—to reach the quarterfinals. She lost that match to France's Marion Bartoli, who would go on from there to win the championship. Still, it was Stephens's second Grand Slam quarterfinals appearance of the year.

Back in the United States after that, she notched another big upset at the Western & Southern Open in Cincinnati in August. She defeated No. 3, Maria Sharapova, in the second round before falling to Jelena Jankovic, who went on to the semifinals.

The Western & Southern Open was one of the key run-up events to the last major of the year, the US Open. Stephens arrived in New York in late August as the fifteenth seed.

She looked great in the first three rounds of the US Open, setting up the much-anticipated rematch with Serena Williams.

This was the first time the two would meet since that fateful day at the Australian tournament. Williams was in the middle of another dominant run. She had been on a twenty-match win streak when Stephens upset her in Australia, but there was to be no upset in New York. Williams, once again No. 1 in the world, breezed past Stephens this time, 6–4, 6–1, on the way to winning her fifth US Open title.

After Williams got her revenge in their fourth-round match, a reporter asked her what Stephens needed to do to improve.

"I don't think she has to work on anything," Williams said. "I think she's at the next level."

Even though Stephens did not have great success in the smaller matches that ended the 2013 season, it proved to be a banner year for her. It was a strange year, to be sure. Not only did Stephens not win any events in 2013, she didn't even reach the final of any events. However, she was one of only three players to advance to at least the fourth round of all four majors.

Because of that consistent success, Stephens finished the year ranked No. 12 in the world. She was the only woman in the top thirty under the age of twenty-two, and she was the second-highest-ranked American behind Serena Williams.

Near the end of 2013, Stephens brought on Paul Annacone to be her new coach. A former pro who was ranked as high as No. 12 in the world during his playing days, Annacone has a very successful track record as a coach—working with two of the all-time best men's champions, Pete Sampras and Roger Federer.

When Annacone started working with Stephens, he immediately noticed what he called "the efficiency of her gifts." He saw the powerful serve and the superior athletic ability that made chasing down tough shots look so easy. "My eyes just kind of popped out of my head," he said.

The sky was the limit for Stephens, coming off that breakthrough season in 2013. That was why her inconsistency in 2014 became magnified. Stephens continued her streak of reaching the fourth round in Grand Slam events by doing so in the Australian Open and again at the French. But that was as far as she got in both those tournaments. The fourth-round streak would be snapped at Wimbledon, when she lost in the first round. After that, it was a second-round departure in the US Open.

By the end of the year, Stephens fell to No. 36 in the world—not bad at all for a twenty-one-year-old, but obviously a disappointment after getting so close to cracking the top ten the year before.

The expectations were high, but again, Stephens refused to let her tennis ranking define her.

Even though she'd eventually cleared the air with Serena Williams in 2013, Stephens meant what she said about Kim Clijsters being her favorite player on the tour. And it wasn't really because of the way she played tennis.

"She's a great competitor, but she's so nice and so sweet," Stephens told *American Way* magazine. "It's hard to find."

Clijsters, who was ranked No. 1 in the world back in 2003, when Stephens was ten years old and just starting to play, retired from tennis in 2007 to start a family. After giving birth to her first child in 2008, she returned to the sport a year later and became the first unranked player ever to win the US Open. In doing so, she also became the first mother to win a Grand Slam event in twenty-nine years.

"She's just done a really good job of balancing her life and priorities," said Stephens, who also prides herself on keeping a healthy work/life balance.

While Stephens was always striving to maintain that kind of balance and not put too much pressure on herself, one thing that was holding her back was a nagging wrist injury that first came about in early 2014. She was able to play through it most of the year but spent much of her time after the 2014 US Open resting and rehabilitating.

"It was tough on me, but things happen, ups and downs," she would later say, reflecting on her inconsistent 2014 season. "I was just happy to get through it."

Still, the wrist was not 100 percent when the 2015 tennis season began, and Stephens did not go far in the Australian Open or any tournaments early in the year. When she got back to the United States in March, however, things started to look up.

Stephens reached the fourth round at Indian Wells, where she lost a tough three-set match to No. 1, Serena Williams. Then, at the Miami Open, she reached the quarterfinals. Along the way, she played her first match against Madison Keys, who was twenty years old at the time and ranked eighteenth in the world. Although Stephens's rank had dropped to No. 45 at the time, this match was being billed as a look into the future of American women's tennis.

Stephens rose to the occasion, easily dismissing Keys, 6–4, 6–2, before losing to Simona Halep, the No. 3 player in the world.

At the French Open in June, Stephens had a double dose of the Williams sisters. She played Venus Williams for the first time and defeated the elder sister in the first round before losing to Serena in the fourth round. It was the furthest Stephens advanced in any of the 2015 Grand Slam events. The rest of the European leg of the 2015 season was inconsistent for her, though she did notch a victory against No. 9, Carla Suarez Navarro, at the Eastbourne International—it was her first win against a top ten opponent in almost two years.

Even though Stephens was No. 35 by the time she returned to the US that summer, she still had the dubious distinction of being the highest-ranked women's player to never reach the final of a WTA event. Going into the Citi Open in Washington, DC, in early August, Stephens had a career record of 0–6 in WTA semifinal matches.

That was about to change.

Despite being unseeded in the tournament,

Stephens defeated No. 2 seed Sam Stosur in the semifinals, 7–6, 6–0, to reach her first WTA final. On August 9, 2015, she earned a 6–1, 6–2 victory over Anastasia Pavlyuchenkova to win her first-ever WTA championship.

In her post-match interview on the court, the first thing Stephens did was say hello to her grandparents. She explained that she always FaceTimed with them on Sundays, and being in the final had disrupted that schedule. Then it sank in.

"I've had a lot of ups and downs," Stephens told the crowd. "Nothing was rushed. Nothing was given to me. I had to work for everything, and it was just nice that all the hard work and everything that I put into it—now I can say that I have a tournament title."

CHAPTER 8

DEALING WITH INJURY

In November 2015, Stephens hired a new coach, Kamau Murray. Unlike her past coaches, who had been professionals themselves and worked with many players, Murray was different. He had been a successful college tennis player after growing up on the South Side of Chicago, but he never played professionally. When he got into coaching, his ambition wasn't to be a mentor to the stars of the game. His greatest desire was to teach the sport he loved to children—especially to underserved children in areas where tennis might not be such an easy option.

Stephens was immediately drawn to Murray, and vice versa. Murray was so good with kids, and Stephens—not yet twenty-three years old— was really just a big kid herself. Murray "got" Stephens. He understood that she had a passion for winning—but that it wasn't the be-all and end-all. He knew the secret to getting the best out of Stephens was to push her sometimes but to allow her to enjoy time off the court.

"I really value how important it is for a [young] woman to be happy," he told *American Way* magazine in 2018. "Happy people win more matches."

With Murray in her corner, that's exactly what she did. In the first four months of 2016, Stephens won three WTA titles—in New Zealand, Mexico, and Charleston, South Carolina.

While she usually played better in the majors than she did in these smaller tournaments, however, she didn't make it out of the third round in either the French Open or Wimbledon.

Part of the reason for those early exits was that she had injured her left foot earlier in the year, but she chose to play through the pain. If it were any other year, she might have taken time off to heal before getting back into serious competition, but there was added incentive in 2016. After narrowly missing out on her chance to compete in the Olympics in 2012, she desperately wanted to make the US team that would be going to Rio de Janeiro for the 2016 Games.

Despite the foot injury, Stephens accomplished her goal and made the Olympics. By the time she got to Rio, however, the foot was so bad that it was a struggle just to walk. But she had made it this far, so she would not be denied the opportunity to represent her country in Olympic action. In a first-round match between unseeded players, she lost in straight sets to Eugenie Bouchard of Canada.

Back home after the Olympics, she focused on the injury. An MRI revealed it was a stress fracture.

After climbing back up the WTA rankings and reaching No. 25, Stephens was told by doctors to shut it down for the rest of the season.

She would miss the US Open that summer, but it could have been worse. Ordered to rest the foot, she essentially had a four-month vacation. She spent time with family and friends, relaxing and binging her favorite TV shows—*Nashville* and *Scandal*. She also spent more time with her boyfriend, professional soccer player Jozy Altidore. Stephens and Altidore, who plays for Toronto FC of major league soccer and is also a member of the US Men's National Team, were actually childhood friends growing up in South Florida. They reconnected in early 2016 and the relationship blossomed. They have become something of a sports "power couple," though they manage to keep their love life private.

By the time January rolled around, Stephens had gone through the longest stretch without playing any tennis since she first took up the sport. She was okay with that, but it was finally time to get back on the court. There was just one problem.

Her first match back was in a tune-up in Sydney before the 2017 Australian Open. But when she started playing, the foot injury returned. This time, rest was not enough. On January 23, Stephens had surgery on the foot.

After the surgery, she was ordered to stay off the foot for three months. For a while, she was confined to a wheelchair. Then she was fitted for a protective boot. The boot had a small extension at the bottom so that if she did need to walk on it, the pressure would not be on the part of her foot that needed to heal. Stephens likened the boot to a "peg leg."

While she wasn't close to actually playing tennis, Stephens wasn't far from the game. She watched a lot of tennis on TV, gaining valuable perspective on what her peers were doing on the court.

She also used this downtime to practice for a

possible career after her playing days were over. Following in the footsteps of so many professional athletes, Stephens decided to get a taste of what it was like to work in the television industry. So she signed on to do some work for the Tennis Channel.

She worked as part of the Tennis Channel's studio team in their production facility in Southern California during the spring tournaments at Indian Wells and Charleston. Veteran Tennis Channel commentator Mary Carillo was very impressed with how easily Stephens carried herself on camera.

"She was just very assured," said Carillo. "Very calm."

During a tennis podcast on the website of the *Daily Telegraph* in London in 2018, Carillo told a story about how Stephens would make fun of her for always getting to work extra early to prepare. While Carillo felt she needed to put in long hours, making sure she covered everything she needed to know, she was very impressed with how Stephens could just show up and be very natural and carefree.

"Finally, she saw me one more time, preposter-ously early and working on my stuff," said Carillo. "And I said, 'Go ahead, make fun of me.' And she said, 'No, I get it. That's your jam.'"

It was clear to Carillo and others that Stephens was in a good place. Not that she wasn't eager to get back on the court and play tennis again. She was. But time off the court turned out to be even more than just what the doctor ordered.

"I obviously wasn't happy to get injured," Stephens told usopen.org later that year. "But it was a good lesson for me. It was a good time to be able to take a break, get my health in order, then just kind of reevaluate my whole entire situation, come back a better player and better person."

Some professional athletes might not have handled the extended time off quite as well. For Stephens, though, it turned out to be the opposite. Having been active on the junior circuit at such a young age—not to mention dealing with the deaths of her father and stepfather—time away from tennis was actually a chance to remind Stephens that she was a carefree twenty-three-year-old.

"It's been fun, actually," she told Tennis Channel's *Beyond the Baseline* podcast in March 2017—just days before her twenty-fourth birthday. "People think it's so depressing—you don't have anything to do, you're so bored. But it definitely hasn't been. I've been able to hang out with friends and family, and live kind of a normal life for the last eight months or so."

That said, Stephens was ready to get back on the court.

"I don't even know what to expect," she said, "but I'm hoping after I come back from the injury that I can play some of the best tennis I've ever played. That's the goal. . . . Just to get back out there—I miss the game, I miss traveling."

Even before the boot on her foot was removed, Stephens was going to physical therapy two hours a day, five days a week. When she finally got the boot off, she was working even harder.

On April 18, 2017, Stephens posted a short video of herself on her Instagram account, slowly walking during a rehab session. The caption read: "Day 1 walking . . . EXCITED!!!!!!!!"

CHAPTER 9

GRAND SLAM AND BEYOND

All in all, the foot injury kept Stephens away from tennis for eleven months. Almost an entire year without competition. When she was finally cleared to play again, at the beginning of the summer of 2017, she could have taken it slowly.

But taking things slowly was not her jam—to borrow an expression Stephens liked to use. Her first tournament back after eleven months: Wimbledon.

When she lost to Eugenie Bouchard in the first round of the 2016 Olympics, her last match before being sidelined, she was ranked No. 28 in the world.

When she arrived in London for Wimbledon, she was down to No. 336. Amazingly, that was nowhere near as low as she would go.

Her grand return didn't last long. Stephens lost her first-round match in straight sets to an unranked opponent. Her next match came three weeks later at the Citi Open in Washington, DC. Her first-round opponent this time was the No. 1 player in the world, Simona Halep. Again, she lost in straight sets.

At that point, 336 wasn't so bad. Her new ranking: No. 957.

Still, the Citi Open did prove to be something of a turning point for Stephens. While she was done after one round in the singles competition, she showed signs of shaking off the rust playing doubles with Bouchard, the Canadian who'd defeated her in the Olympics. Stephens and Bouchard teamed up to reach the finals of the doubles competition at the Citi.

After that, Stephens began to look like Stephens again. In both tournaments she entered in August prior to the US Open, she reached the semifinals. Along the way, she notched victories over ranked opponents Angelique Kerber and Petra Kvitova—serving notice that she could be a factor in the last major of the season.

After her precipitous fall in the rankings, Stephens was up to No. 83 when she arrived in New York for the 2017 US Open. Still, the entry deadline for the Open was a month before, so she had to use a "protected ranking" to be in the main draw of the competition. When a player misses at least six months due to injury, they can use the protected ranking no more than twice to be able to enter a major based on their ranking before the injury.

It didn't take long for her to make her presence felt. Her opening-round win over Roberta Vinci was her first victory at the Open in three years. She never looked back.

Six wins later—including victories over No. 9, Venus Williams, in the semifinals and No. 15, Madison Keys, in the final—and Sloane Stephens was crowned women's champion of the 2017 US Open.

Keys had been one of Stephens's best friends on the WTA tour for years. When Stephens sealed the victory in her greatest achievement to date, the two pros embraced at center court.

"We've known each other for a long time, and we just wanted to share that moment with each other," Keys said. "I think what she's done is absolutely amazing. When she made her semifinal run in Australia, we all saw how great she was. Sloane has always had the talent."

And, finally, she had a Grand Slam title to show for it. For accomplishing that feat after missing the first half of the year with her foot injury, Stephens was named WTA Comeback Player of the Year.

In winning the Open, Stephens became the first American player—male or female—besides the

Williams sisters to win a major tournament singles title in fourteen years. That fact alone raised expectations tremendously.

At the post-match press conference after the Open victory, a reporter asked her if the win put her on a different level.

"I don't think of it that way," she said. "If anything, I'm still working my way back. I mean I just happen to be—my ranking is a little higher, but if you think about it, five weeks ago, I was like, nine-hundred-and-something, wasn't really a threat. I'm just going to keep going with that and ride that wave for as long as I can."

But the expectations did weigh on her, and the wave became more of a wipeout. In tournaments that followed the US Open, she lost eight straight matches.

"I felt really disappointed when I wasn't delivering, and that kind of brought me down more than it would have normally," she told *Time* magazine.

What most people didn't realize was that Stephens had a minor knee injury She could have taken a break until she was 100 percent healthy, but she didn't want to endure another prolonged stretch of time away from the game.

She did, however, keep a lighter schedule late in 2017 so that she could focus on her studies. She was taking online college classes through Indiana University East, and by the end of the year she earned her bachelor's degree in communications.

If some people questioned her desire because she was skipping practice to focus on schoolwork, Stephens could care less.

"Bro, I've got to graduate," she said in the *Time* magazine interview. "This is important, okay."

Her eighth consecutive loss came at the Australian Open in early 2018. She finally broke the losing streak with a first-round win in Acapulco, Mexico. She lost in the quarterfinals of that tournament, but it appeared the ship had been righted. One month later, close to home at the Miami Open, Stephens defeated three top-ten opponents—including No. 5, Jelena Ostapenko of Latvia, in the final. By winning the title, Stephens maintained her streak of never having lost once she got to the final of a tournament.

For the first time in her career, Stephens cracked the top ten in the world rankings, climbing to No. 9.

But her streak of never losing in a final ended when she was defeated by Simona Halep at the 2018 French Open. True to her nature, though, she wasn't as disappointed about the loss as she was happy for Halep, who was stunned to win her first Grand Slam event.

Halep didn't know what to do after being interviewed on TV after the match. It was Stephens who nudged her to take the trophy and hoist it over her head.

Once again, it fueled the perception that Stephens didn't care enough. Maybe it's okay to give your opponent a little credit in the media after losing a big match. It's okay to shake hands and congratulate the person who just defeated you. But to show outright joy for your vanquisher? To be all smiles in the face of losing? That's just not how it's done, is it?

"Sportswriters want to see the player implode and have a John McEnroe sort of experience," Kamau Murray, Stephens's coach since 2015, told *American Way* magazine. McEnroe, of course, is the Hall of Fame tennis player who is famously known for his on-court outbursts and heated exchanges with umpires. "Her approach to the game is very healthy. She realizes, as a black female, there are a lot of girls in a worse-off position. That's helped her move on."

CHAPTER 10

HELPING OTHERS

It's true that Sloane Stephens and tennis legend Serena Williams had a well-publicized feud in 2013, and perhaps there is some truth to the story about Stephens becoming disillusioned when she was a young girl waiting in vain for Williams to autograph her poster. But there is no denying the impact Serena Williams and her older sister Venus had on Stephens when she was growing up.

"They've set the bar so high," Stephens told the US Tennis Association in a video promoting Black History Month. "Growing up as a little black girl watching them has been so cool. I've been lucky to play with them, and not only watch them on TV but actually be in the same tournaments as them, play against them. I think that's been one of the coolest things of my playing career, playing against two of the greatest women ever to play—that happen to be African American."

Since Venus and Serena Williams burst onto the tennis scene in the late 1990s, the sport has witnessed the "Williams Effect"—a growth in the popularity of tennis in the African American community, a demographic that typically did not embrace the sport. One of the main reasons for that is because there are usually not many opportunities to play tennis in underserved communities where the population is predominantly African American.

The Williams sisters themselves came from one such community: Compton, California. It wasn't until their father moved them to South Florida that they got more professional training and were entering major competitions.

Stephens was more fortunate than most. She lived across the street from a tennis club and had the opportunity to play tennis as a nine-year-old in the place where her mother and stepfather were members.

Now that she has risen to a level of prominence in her sport, Stephens relishes the chance to help kids who don't have the same opportunities she had. She launched the Sloane Stephens Foundation, which, among other things, works to improve conditions for kids in underserved areas of the country to play tennis.

"If I can inspire one person to play tennis, I think that's pretty cool," she said. "And that's what I get out of my foundation. The kids there have no idea who I am, have no idea that I've won a Grand Slam or what that even means. But they just know that I come every Saturday and play tennis with them and feed them doughnuts, stuff like that, and I'm a really cool person to be around. That's kind of given me a little bit more drive, because I know I can help people outside of my sport—not just kids that want to play tennis."

Stephens launched the foundation in 2013, long before she was a Grand Slam champion. When she was nursing her foot injury at the end of 2016 into the first half of 2017, she took advantage of that downtime to work as much as possible with kids through the foundation.

"It really gave me something to look forward to every day," Stephens told Tennis.com a year after coming back from the injury. "Without that I probably couldn't be as happy as I am on court right now."

Stephens lived in Southern California at the time. She would visit after-school programs in Compton, California, during the week and host local clinics on Saturdays.

"No matter what, my priority is always going to

be the kids and the foundation," she said. "When I was sad and I was upset that I couldn't play, the kids really put a smile on my face. The time that I was injured, I was able to give my full self to these kids. That really kept me going over the six months that I was at home."

Stephens may have gained an appreciation for working with kids from her coach, Kamau Murray. While her previous coaches were former professionals themselves, Murray was far less connected to the pro ranks. The Chicago native wasn't as concerned about working with a Grand Slam contender as he was helping introduce the sport to kids who might otherwise never play tennis at all. And that dedication to kids in impoverished communities was part of what sold Stephens on Murray in the first place.

"One of the most powerful components of their relationship is that Sloane admires and respects what Kamau does in Chicago," her mother told the

Undefeated website in 2018, when Murray opened a youth tennis center for underserved kids on the city's South Side. "And for Kamau, I think he realizes that Sloane needs not only a coach so that she can continue to develop, but she needs mentoring. Finding that balance is challenging for any coach. It was a perfect storm for Kamau and Sloane. His junior program gave him the right skill set for her."

And so Stephens is a frequent guest at Murray's $15 million facility in Chicago. She's also spent time working with youth in Compton, California, the same community where the Williams sisters came from. Stephens works with the Compton Unified School District, offering programs in twenty-three locations across the city. In addition to giving children the opportunity to participate, she fully understands how important it is for them to have a role model.

"I think more can always be done," Stephens

said during an appearance on "We Need to Talk" on CBS Sports Network. "It's definitely hard. I grew up across the street from a club, so I played. Accessibility is key.

"If you give a kid an opportunity, you give them a racquet, you give them a ball, you show them, they will fall in love with tennis. My mission is to make sure that all the kids in Compton are able to play tennis. That area is small, but if I can have an impact on those kids, eventually I'll get through to more kids and more kids and more kids, and make sure that the kids know what they have in front of them and what tools tennis can give them. I think just giving the opportunity, even a small one, can go so far. Tennis has given me amazing opportunities in my life, and I think that every kid should have the same opportunity."

In addition to her work in Compton, Stephens has made a difference in Fresno, California, where she grew up. She helps fund tennis programs at

Edison-Bethune Charter Academy, introducing children to the sport.

Through the Fresno County Office of Education, Stephens has helped expand tennis programs at other local elementary and middle schools, particularly for students from economically disadvantaged communities.

"I'm from Fresno, so it feels really good to participate in the development of elementary-school-aged kids, not just with tennis, but with choosing a healthy lifestyle," Stephens told the *Fresno Bee* in 2015. "It's an honor to help in any way I can."

Stephens also got closely involved with a charity called Soles4Souls, which collects sneakers and other athletic apparel and distributes it to those in need. She can often be seen at various matches around the world trolling the athletic facilities where her peers are training, and asking them to donate their used sneakers.

"Soles4Souls is a great charity to give back to, and it helps tons of people," Stephens said prior to the 2017 Connecticut Open. At the 2016 Connecticut Open alone, she helped the organization collect more than five hundred pounds' worth of sneakers to donate.

CHAPTER 11

SLOANE'S LEGACY

Although Stephens lost in the first round at Wimbledon in 2018, her success in reaching the final at the French Open earlier in the year helped her reach a career-high ranking of No. 3 in the world. She had a strong summer back in the United States, building up to her return to New York—where she hoped to defend her US Open title.

Stephens reached the quarterfinals, where she faced Anastasija Sevastova—the same opponent she'd played in the quarterfinals at the 2017 US Open. This time, however, the results were different. On a brutally hot day in Flushing Meadows, Stephens lost in straight sets to Sevastova, abruptly ending her bid for a second straight US Open crown.

In typical Sloane Stephens fashion, she chose to look at the positive side. She could have really botched her title defense by losing in the first round, but that didn't happen. She won four matches, including a third-round win against two-time Australian Open champ Victoria Azarenka and a fourth-round victory against No. 15, Elise Mertens, who had defeated Stephens just three weeks earlier at the Western & Southern Open.

In a press conference following her loss to Sevastova, she said, "I can be proud of a lot of things that happened . . . so I'm not going to dwell on it. Just keep building. There's four more tournaments left. I'm just going to try to play the rest of the season as hard as I can and hopefully have some more good results."

That's exactly what happened. Unlike 2017,

when Stephens went into a bad slump following the US Open, she finished 2018 on a high note. While she didn't win any titles, she reached the championship match of the WTA Finals in Singapore—defeating four top-ten-ranked opponents before falling to Elina Svitolina.

Paul Annacone, Stephens's former coach, was in Singapore covering the WTA Finals for the Tennis Channel. He could tell that Stephens had matured as a player, that she now seemed to have what it took to avoid the kind of slumps she had endured in the past.

"It used to be that when she lost a few matches she would get derailed for a while," Annacone said. "Now she may go through some losing streaks, but it doesn't really crush her confidence. She can bounce back pretty quickly.

"I don't think she's accepting mediocrity."

By the end of 2018, Stephens was ranked No. 6 in the world. A few months into 2019, she had something else to celebrate: On April 29, Stephens announced on Instagram that she got engaged to marry longtime boyfriend, Jozy Altidore.

Still just twenty-five years old at the time, she had plenty of tennis ahead of her—but she was also thinking about life after tennis. And while she is proud of her accomplishments on the court, it's clear she envisions a legacy that goes beyond the game of tennis. With a college degree already in hand, she began taking courses to earn an MBA—master of business administration. She became more involved in some of the business deals her representatives were negotiating.

"I'd much rather be able to tell my kids, 'Yeah, Mommy got a degree, Mommy did this,'" she said. "After tennis I'm going to—God willing—be a parent and run a business. Tennis careers are not that long."

That doesn't mean her tennis career is ending anytime soon, however. Venus and Serena Williams are both still going strong at ages thirty-nine and thirty-eight, respectively. If Stephens plays another ten years, it's easy to imagine she will add more Grand Slam titles to her already successful résumé.

It took a little longer than expected, but all those "Heir Apparent" stories that were written when Stephens beat Serena at the 2013 Australian Open quarterfinals are finally true. With the Williams sisters nearing the tail end of their careers, Stephens is becoming the new face of women's tennis in America. That status has earned her major endorsement deals with high-profile brands such as Nike, American Express, and Mercedes-Benz, just to name a few.

Following in the footsteps of Venus and Serena, Stephens has become a role model and inspiration for African American girls. It's a responsibility that can put a lot of pressure on her, but she embraces it.

What's interesting about the comparisons to the Williams sisters is that Stephens's childhood has given her a much different perspective.

Whereas the Williams sisters grew up with a father, Richard Williams, who drove them hard to become tennis stars and was an ever-present part of their lives, Stephens grew up without her father—and then had to come to terms with his tragic death not long after the two finally connected.

Having dealt with the loss of both her biological father and her stepfather—who was instrumental in getting her started in tennis—at such a young age has a lot to do with how Stephens handles her career. Losing a tennis match, after all, is nothing like losing a father.

"I play a sport for a living. I don't, like, operate on people," Stephens told usopen.org during her title run in 2017. "This is not life or death. I think it's hard to realize that when you're out there playing because there's a lot riding on it: prize money, points, so many things go into it. I think I have it pretty good. I think once I realized that, I was, like: life is actually really very good."

Because of that perspective, Stephens is not afraid to lose, and that fearlessness on the court helps her stay loose and confident. It doesn't mean there aren't some tough times to deal with. There are plenty of ups and downs every year on the tennis tour. The fact of the matter is that Stephens refuses to let herself get too down.

And there are still some in the tennis world who aren't comfortable with that disposition. Those who don't fully understand where she's coming from still speculate that Stephens just doesn't care enough about winning. They don't understand why she isn't more upset when she loses a match.

Perspective has also helped Stephens to block out the negative comments and doubts.

"Everyone always has something to say," she told *Sports Illustrated* in March 2018. "Like when I was injured, everyone said, 'Is she ever going to play again? Is she ever gonna be the same as she was before?' Now it's, Am I ever going to win another Grand Slam? You have to kind of just set them aside. Because at the end of the day you can only control what you can control. You can only control yourself."

Despite having lost important people in her life, Stephens recognizes that she has strong support from her family and close friends. She knows there is pressure on her to remain a positive role model for female athletes and she does so by taking one day at a time, steadily moving forward in her career.

And always smiling.

"I'm in a good place," Stephens told *Time* magazine in September 2018. "People say, 'Oh, you're inconsistent, you're this, you're that.' Whatever. When I retire from tennis, I'll be able to look back and say I did it the way I wanted to do it. I was just playing. And I was just making sure I was happy along the way."

SOURCES

ABC Action News. "Tennis Pro Sloane Stephens Has Valley Roots." ABC News, January 24, 2013. https://abc30.com/archive/8966010/.

Anteola, Bryant-Jon. "She Beat Venus to Reach the US Open Final: A Look at Sloane Stephens' Fresno Ties." *Fresno Bee*, September 7, 2017. https://www.fresnobee.com/sports/article171946537.html.

Becco, Laine Bergeson. "Sloane Stephens: Rising Star." Experience Life (website), November 2013. https://experiencelife.com/article/sloane-stephens-rising-star/.

Bembry, Jerry. "Sloane Stephens' Fear of Bugs and Other Things to Know about Her." The Undefeated, September 7, 2017. https://theundefeated.com /features/us-open-sloane-stephens-fear-of-bugs -and-other-things-to-know-about-her/.

Bembry, Jerry. "Sloane Stephens Joins Elite Company with Her US Open Victory." The Undefeated, September 10, 2017. https://theundefeated.com /features/sloane-stephens-joins-elite-company -with-her-us-open-victory/.

Bodo, Peter. "Watch Out, Singapore Field: Sloane Stephens Has Something to Prove." ESPN.com, October 24, 2018. http://www.espn.com/tennis /story/_/id/25071624/tennis-watch-singapore-field -sloane-stephens-mission.

Cogan, Marin. "They Want Another Serena." ESPN the Magazine, May 6, 2013. http://www.espn.com/espnw

/news-commentary/article/9227331/sloane-stephens
-intent-doing-more-beating-serena-williams-espn
-magazine.

Creveling, Mallory. "How Sloane Stephens Trains, Eats,
and Mentally Prepares to Crush the Competition." *Shape*,
August 24, 2018. https://www.shape.com/celebrities
/interviews/sloane-stephens-training-diet-self-love
-2018-us-open.

Crouse, Karen. "For a Rising Star, a Connection, Then
Dealing with Loss." *New York Times*, September 4, 2009.
https://www.nytimes.com/2009/09/05/sports/tennis
/05stephens.html?scp=1&sq=sloane%20stephens&st=cse.

Evans, Kelley D. "US Open Champion Sloane Stephens
Is Teaching Kids How to Play the Game." The
Undefeated, April 18, 2018. https://theundefeated
.com/features/us-open-champion-sloane-stephens
-rebuilding-tennis-courts-in-compton/.

Goodman, Lizzy. "Is Sloane Stephens the Future of American Tennis?" *Elle*, July 16, 2014. https://www .elle.com/culture/career-politics/a12790/sloane -stephens-profile/.

Gregory, Sean. "Serena's Heir." *Time*, June 3, 2013. http://content.time.com/time/subscriber/article /0,33009,2144119-2,00.html.

Gregory, Sean. "US Open Champion Sloane Stephens Is Set to Defend Her Title—and Defy Her Critics." *Time*, August 23, 2018. http://time.com/5375705 /sloane-stephens/.

Henley, Blair. "Sloane Stephens Ready to Sparkle in 2013." Tennis Now, December 19, 2012. http://www .tennisnow.com/News/Featured-News/Sloane -Stephens-Ready-to-Sparkle-in-2013.aspx.

Kindelan, Katie. "Serena and Venus Williams Reign at the US Open: Inside the 'Williams Effect' on Tennis." ABC News Radio, August 29, 2018. https://abcnews .go.com/GMA/News/serena-venus-williams-reign -us-open-inside-williams/story?id=57424231.

Lewis, Colette. "Lauren Davis Upsets Third Seed Babos; Stephens Advances in Three Sets at US Open Junior Championships." Tennis Kalamazoo, September 9, 2009. http://tenniskalamazoo.blogspot .com/2009/09/lauren-davis-upsets-third-seed-babos .html.

Marshall, Ashley. "50 for 50: Sloane Stephens, 2017 Women's Singles Champion." usopen.org, February 28, 2018. https://www.usopen.org/en_US /news/articles/2018-02-28/50_for_50_sloane_stephens _2017_womens_singles_champion.html.

Mendell, David. "He Coached Sloane Stephens to a US Open Title, but Kamau Murray's Big Goal Is a Youth Tennis Center in Chicago." The Undefeated, February 23, 2018. https://theundefeated.com/features/sloane-stephens-coach-kamau-murray-youth-tennis-center-in-chicago/.

Nguyen, Courtney. "Sloane Stephens Takes Blame, Declares Peace with Serena Williams in Tweet." *Sports Illustrated*, May 7, 2013. https://www.si.com/node/421701.

Oddo, Chris. "Chris Evert Says Sloane Stephens Lacks Hunger." Tennis Now, August 27, 2014. http://www.tennisnow.com/News/-Chris-Evert-Says-Sloane-Stephens-Lacks-Hunger.aspx.

Pantic, Nina. "Stephens Says Her Foundation Helped Her Through Injury." Tennis.com, June 29, 2018. http://baseline.tennis.com/article/74833/sloane-stephens-foundation-kids-helped-injury.

Powell, Shaun. "A Father's Pride." Sports on Earth, August 20, 2013. http://www.sportsonearth.com /article/57519810/sloane-stephens-father-john -new-england-patriots-running-back.

Price, S. L. "The Complex Rise of Sloane Stephens." *Sports Illustrated*, September 12, 2017. https://www .si.com/tennis/2017/09/12/sloane-stephens -us-open-title-family-kamau-murray-injury -recovery.

Reilly, Phoebe. "For Tennis Star Sloane Stephens, Life Is More than Just a Series of Games." *American Way*, August 2018. https://magazines.aa.com/en /features/2018/07/break-points.

Schlecht, Neil. "Sloane Stephens: Life Is Good." usopen.org, September 5, 2017. https://www.usopen .org/en_US/news/articles/2017-09-05/2017-09-03 _sloane_stephens_life_is_good.html.

Telegraph Sport. "What French Open Finalist Sloane Stephens Is Really Like." Podcast, The Telegraph (website), June 9, 2018. https://www.telegraph.co.uk /tennis/2018/06/09/tennis-podcast-french-open -finalist-sloane-stephens-really-like/.

Thomas, Louisa. "Can Sloane Stephens Repeat Her US Open Triumph?" *Vogue*, August 16, 2018. https://www .vogue.com/article/sloane-stephens-us-open-vogue -september-2018-issue.

Wertheim, Jon. "Sloane Stephens." *Beyond the Baseline* podcast, Tennis Channel, March 9, 2017. http://thetennischannel.com/reporters/jon-wertheim /jon-wertheim-beyond-the-baseline-podcast-sloane -stephens.

ABOUT THE AUTHOR

Craig Ellenport is a sports journalist who has written more than a dozen books. During his thirty-year career, he has covered the NBA, NFL, NHL, MLB, college football, and tennis.